Contents

HOW DO WE KNOW ABOUT OUR PAST?

THE HISTORY JIGSAW

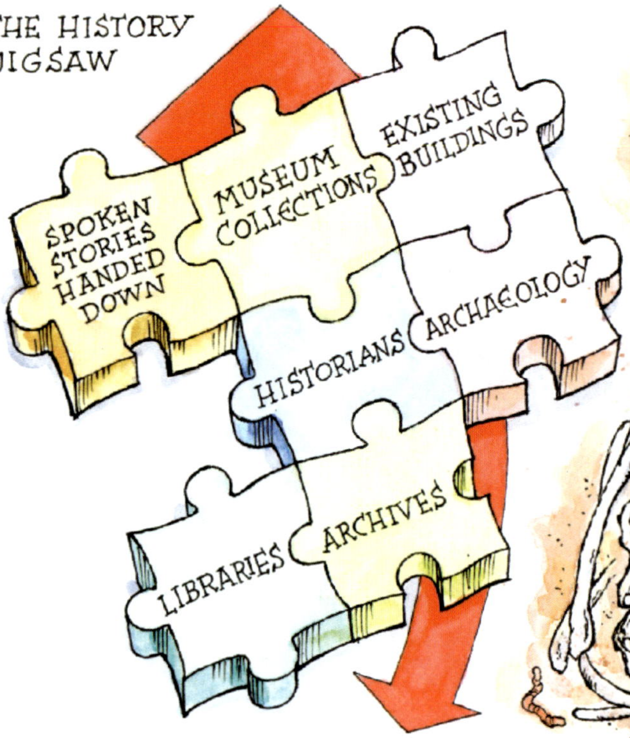

WITH NO PHOTOS, FILMS, TV OR NEWSPAPERS FROM LONG AGO, IT IS HARD TO FIND OUT ABOUT THE PAST...

CLUES from archaeology, documents, maps, books, standing buildings and museum objects are called **sources**.

DOCUMENTS which include manuscripts, chronicles and maps are valuable **evidence** and are kept in special stores called **archives**. **Libraries** also look after ancient books.

MUSEUMS collect interesting objects.

ARCHAEOLOGISTS try to find and date lost sources by digging (excavation). They find old buildings, bones, pottery tools, coins, jewellery, pollen seeds and wood.

ALL THE SPECIALISTS GATHER EVIDENCE TO HELP CREATE A STORY OF THE PAST.

WITH NEW DISCOVERIES, IDEAS ABOUT OUR PAST ARE UPDATED.

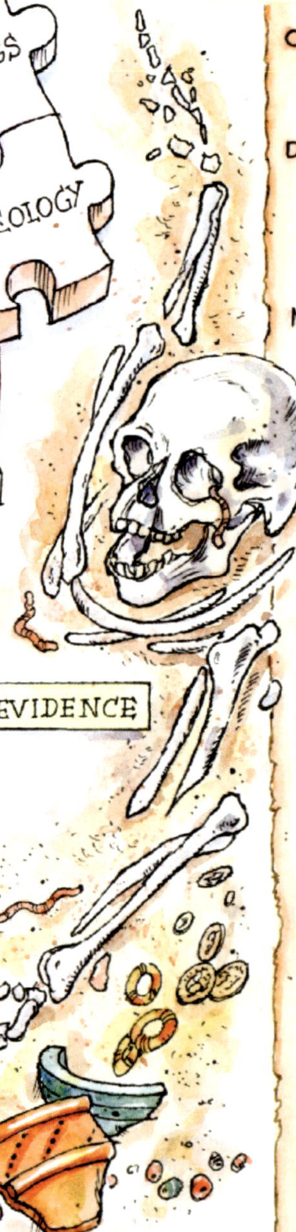

WHAT WE KNOW BASED ON REAL EVIDENCE

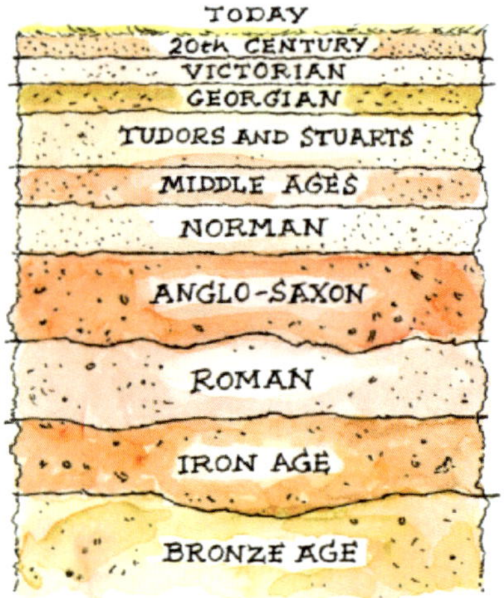

A CANTERBURY ARCHAEOLOGICAL DIG

CANTERBURY BEFORE AUGUSTINE

IRON AGE

PEOPLE HAVE LIVED in this area for thousands of years.

Canterbury is sited at a place where it was easy to cross the River Stour.

On higher ground to the west was the Iron Age hill fort of Bigbury.

When the Romans arrived in AD 43 they found an Iron Age settlement.

ROMAN

THE ROMANS built a fine town at Canterbury which they called Durovernum Cantiacorum.

There were many important buildings such as the forum, temple and theatre.

Archaeologists have found many high-quality Roman artifacts.

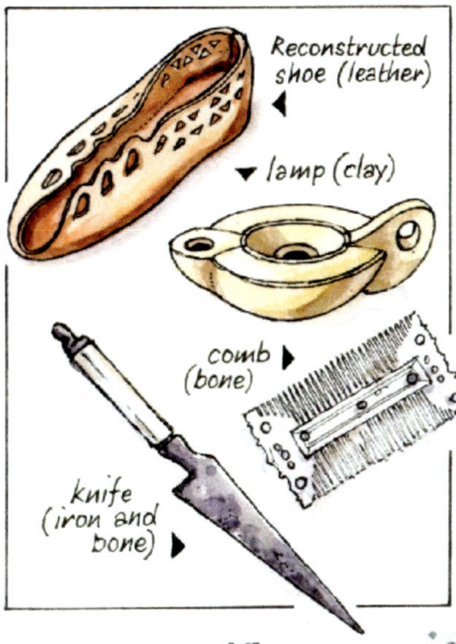

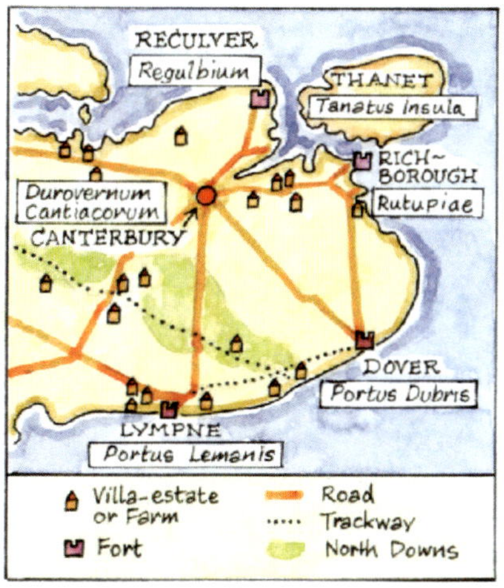

▲ Roman roads in East Kent

The Roman army left Britain around AD 410 and their government stopped working. The buildings in Canterbury began to fall down and trees grew in the streets.

NEW SETTLERS

DIFFERENT PEOPLE came to Canterbury – Jutes, Angles, Franks and Saxons. They built wooden houses within the ruined Roman town. Later on they called their settlement Cantwaraburgh (the stronghold of the people of Kent).

We now call it Canterbury.

AUGUSTINE'S MISSION TO KENT

Augustine and his 40 companions travelled from Rome to Kent and landed on the Isle of Thanet in AD 597.

AUGUSTINE, a monk was sent by Pope Gregory to Kent to convert the Anglo-Saxons to Christianity.

There were already some Christians mainly in the West and North of the British Isles.

IN KENT, King Aethelbert was a pagan but Queen Bertha his wife and her followers were Christians.

She went to the little church of St Martin's to pray.

St Martin's had Roman origins.

KING AETHELBERT WELCOMES AUGUSTINE

Following their meeting, Aethelbert invited the churchmen to stay in Canterbury.

A FEW YEARS LATER King Aethelbert became a Christian and was baptised by Augustine. Others followed the King's example. The King gave Augustine land at Canterbury to build a cathedral and to establish a monastery.

Augustine was the first Archbishop of Canterbury.

THE ANGLO-SAXONS IN CANTERBURY

BETWEEN AD 600 AND AD 800 CANTERBURY WAS PROBABLY THE MAIN SETTLEMENT IN KENT AND BY AD 800 WAS CALLED CANTWARABURGH.

▲ Anglo-Saxon houses in amongst the ruins of the Roman city. A drawing of part of Anglo-Saxon Canterbury around AD 740.

Craftsfolk came to Canterbury: potters, bone-workers, jewellers and bead-makers.

Coins were made at the Royal Mint from about AD 650.

Not to scale

Anglo-Saxon buckle, beads and pendant. These local artefacts were found by archaeologists.

Anglo-Saxon Canterbury about AD 700 ▶

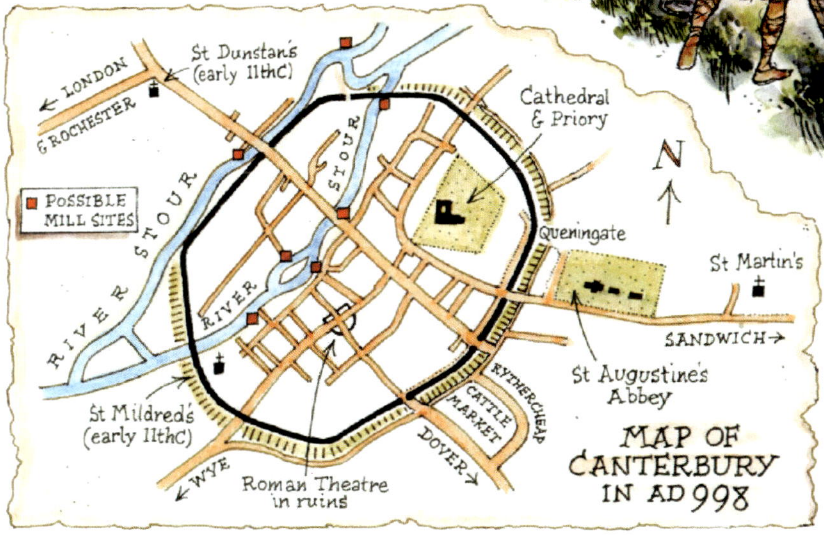

MAP OF CANTERBURY IN AD 998

CANTERBURY was a wealthy city because merchants and traders from other parts of England and continental Europe came to buy and sell goods.

There were several markets. The cattle market at Rythercheap was between St George's and Dover Street.

Millers ground corn into flour to make bread at watermills on the River Stour.

By AD 998 there were probably around 5000 people living here.

ST AUGUSTINE'S ABBEY

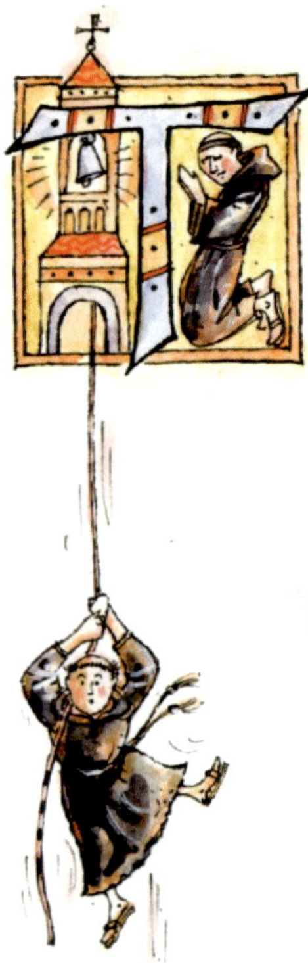

THE ABBEY was founded outside the city walls in around AD 597 by Augustine on land given to him by King Aethelbert.

The King also gave Augustine an old Roman church within the city walls which was to become the cathedral (Christ Church).

THE MONKS lived by a strict code...

...and a daily timetable of prayer.

An example of an illustrated manuscript

Monks were men who wanted to live their lives worshipping God in a closed community.

The monks followed the rule of St Benedict written by Benedict of Nursia and spent much of their time praying in the church. There were also places to sleep (dormitory), eat (refectory) and write (scriptorium). By about AD 1500 the library had perhaps 2000 hand-written books on scripture, law, music, medicine and astronomy.

THE MONASTERIES of ST AUGUSTINE'S ABBEY and CHRIST CHURCH PRIORY were famous as centres of European learning and scholarship long before universities existed.

VIKINGS COME TO CANTERBURY

BETWEEN AD 800 AND AD 900 VIKINGS FROM DENMARK ATTACKED SEVERAL MONASTERIES ALONG THE KENT COAST.

VIKINGS SACKED LYMINGE NUNNERY. Nuns from Lyminge fled to Canterbury because they thought it would be safer.

Archaeologists think they might have found the place where the nuns lived in Canterbury. On the "Old Tannery" site near St Mildred's church.

VERY FEW VIKING REMAINS HAVE BEEN FOUND IN KENT.

A Danish style 10th C. knife. Canterbury Museum

CANTERBURY was also raided by Vikings several times. The worst attack was in 1011. The townspeople fought bravely but could not stop the Vikings taking the city. Many people were killed and the Vikings took all the monks and nuns prisoner. They also captured Alphege the archbishop.

The death of Archbishop Alphege

THE VIKINGS took Alphege to Greenwich and demanded a huge ransom. Alphege refused as he knew his people could not afford it. The Vikings carried out their threat to kill him and did so at a feast on Easter Sunday when they pelted him with ox bones.

To save him from further suffering a Viking killed him with a single axe-blow to the head. As a martyr he became a saint and his body was returned to Canterbury cathedral.

THE CULT OF SAINTS BEFORE BECKET

AS WELL AS St Augustine other early archbishops and several Kentish kings were buried in the church at St Augustine's Abbey.

MANY PEOPLE BELIEVED that these archbishops and kings were holy men. There were holy women too. These royal ladies founded monasteries or nunneries and often became abbesses. Holy men and women were called saints and their burial places were visited by pilgrims long before the martyrdom of Thomas Becket.

The relics of St Mildred are carried into St Augustine's Abbey by the Abbot and monks in AD 1030.

ONE OF THESE SAINTLY WOMEN, called St Mildred, was buried at her monastery in Minster-in-Thanet. In the tenth century her monastery was attacked by the Vikings.

THE NUNS may have come to Canterbury to take shelter before returning to Thanet. According to the monks of St Augustine's, they brought her body from Minster to their church in Canterbury in AD 1030.

WHEN THEY had finished building their new church in AD 1091, the monks moved the bodies of all their saints, including St Augustine and St Mildred, to beautifully decorated new shrines in the east end of their church.

CANTERBURY CATHEDRAL also had the shrines of several saintly archbishops including St Dunstan *(left)* and St Alphege

ST DUNSTAN and the DEVIL

IN THE eleventh century, a monk at the cathedral wrote what are called the "lives" of the saints. He said that St Dunstan had caught the devil by the nose with a pair of pliers.

PILGRIMS CAME TO VISIT SHRINES at Canterbury Cathedral and at St Augustine's Abbey. Among the parish churches of Canterbury are those of St Mildred, St Dunstan and St Alphege.

THE NORMANS ARRIVE

AFTER DEFEATING King Harold at the Battle of Hastings in 1066, Duke William marched with his army to Canterbury on his way to London.

The city surrendered to him. To control the Anglo-Saxons William ordered his soldiers to build a wooden tower on a big earth mound. It was surrounded by a wooden fence and a deep ditch- the first castle.

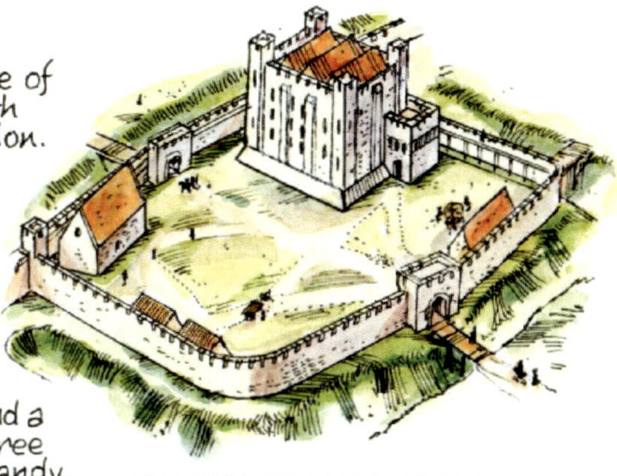

THE NORMAN CASTLE OF 1090.

A SECOND STONE CASTLE was built around 1090 when the Conqueror's son William Rufus was king. It was one of the biggest castles in England at the time. Around the outside was a stone wall and a ditch. The main building was a great stone tower or keep which had three floors. Stone was brought from Maidstone, the Isle of Wight and Normandy. The builders also used stone from the Roman ruins nearby.

The castle keep is still here today.

NORMAN CANTERBURY IN 1170.

LANFRANC

AS PART of his plan to control England, William brought over a monk called Lanfranc from Bec in Normandy who was made Archbishop in 1070.

The cathedral had burnt down three years earlier, so Lanfranc replaced it with a new larger church. Like King William Lanfranc was a great builder, constructing new priory buildings for the monks made from Norman stone.

THE NEW CATHEDRAL

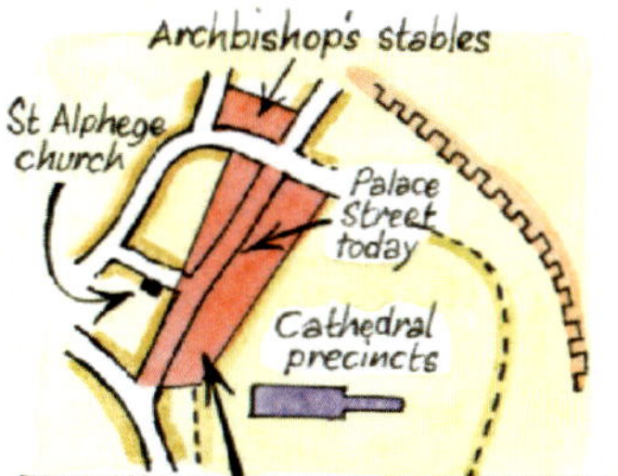

ARCHBISHOP'S PALACE enclosing road and so diverting it - now Called Palace Street.

ARCHBISHOP LANFRANC changed the street pattern in Palace Street. Several houses were knocked down so that he could build a new archbishop's palace. Perhaps because of this he also built two hospitals, one for lepers at Harbledown and one for the sick poor just outside the city's Northgate. Both hospitals still exist, but the elderly people who live there now do not live in Lanfranc's buildings, though parts of the chapels may date from Lanfranc's time.

ST JOHN'S HOSPITAL

THE FAMOUS **BAYEUX TAPESTRY** may well have been made by needlewomen in Canterbury under the orders of Norman Bishop Odo.

CANTERBURY WITHIN EAST KENT

CANTERBURY is in a river valley. The Forest of Blean lies to the North.

To the South there is a large area of Downland. The river valley and Downs are good land for farming.

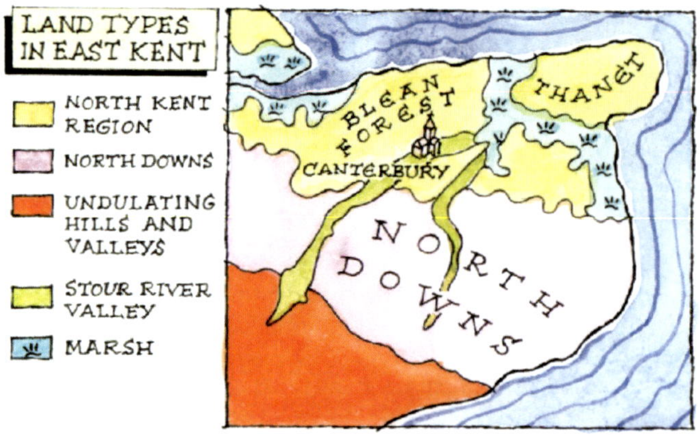

THE GREAT STOUR

THIS RIVER WAS VERY IMPORTANT FOR THE DEVELOPMENT OF CANTERBURY. IT PROVIDED A WAY TO THE WANTSUM CHANNEL AND THEN OUT TO SEA.

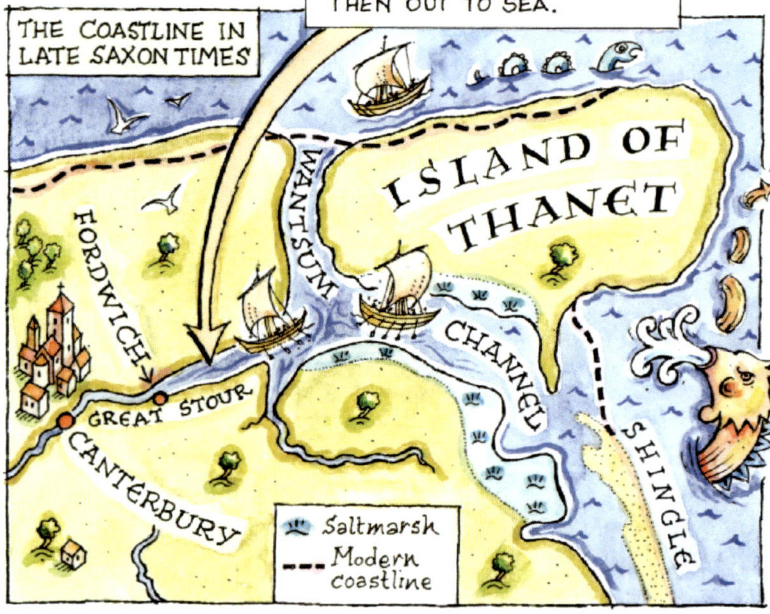

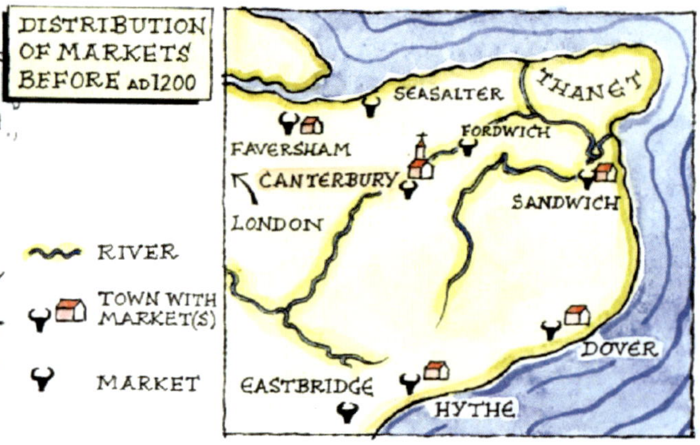

FORDWICH ~ CANTERBURY'S PORT

IN THE LATE 11th.C large amounts of Caen stone from Normandy were brought by boat up the Great Stour river to Fordwich - some 2 miles due east of Canterbury.
It was probably off-loaded there and brought by cart to the city.

The stone was used by the archbishop, the king and the monks at St Augustine's Abbey. It was an expensive high-quality stone and its use showed everyone how important Canterbury was to the king and to the church.

An artist's impression of Canterbury's own port of Fordwich in AD 1100.

CANTERBURY IN THE TIME OF BECKET

MANY DIFFERENT TYPES of craftsmen and craftswomen worked in Canterbury.

They produced goods for other citizens and for the monks and nuns.

THE AUGUSTINIAN CANONS were regular priests who came to Canterbury in 1133. Their base was called St Gregory's Priory where they followed the rule of St Augustine of Hippo.

Soon after the canons arrived there was a serious fire which destroyed many buildings.

The canons received gifts of land and money from the local people and the archbishop. This meant they could build a new priory.

A tannery was a very smelly workshop where leather was cured. Tanneries were sited along the River Stour as water was needed in the process.

Masons, carpenters and others working on St Gregory's Priory.

TERRIC THE GOLDSMITH'S WORKSHOP

ONE OF the goldsmiths who worked in 12th century Canterbury was called Terric. Archaeologists have found his workshop in the Longmarket area.

It contained several crucibles (or melting pots) used to melt down gold and silver.

WEAVING

DYEING

CLOTHMAKING

AS WELL AS many immigrant workers from Europe, several Jewish families lived in the area which included Jewry Lane.
They were allowed to work as money lenders by the Church and some became very rich, living in houses made of stone rather than wood.

THOMAS BECKET

THOMAS BECKET became King Henry II's chancellor in 1155 and Archbishop of Canterbury in 1162.

KING HENRY expected his old friend would help to change the law to favour the King against the Church but Thomas did not agree with the King's ideas and they quarrelled.

FOR THE GOOD of the Church, Thomas left England. Six years later he returned from exile and the people of Canterbury flocked to see him.

Becket returns from France and lands at Sandwich. ▼

ALMOST IMMEDIATELY Thomas angered the king again because he excommunicated (expelled from the Church) certain barons and bishops who supported Henry.

IN 1170 the king was in France celebrating Christmas. He was annoyed and is supposed to have said: ....

WHILST HENRY'S COURT was celebrating Christmas, four of his knights: **WILLIAM DE TRACY, REGINALD FITZURSE, RICHARD LE BRET** and **HUGH DE MOREVILLE** travelled from France to Canterbury.

WHEN THE KNIGHTS met Becket at the cathedral, there was a quarrel and they killed him.

THE MARTYRDOM OF BECKET

THE MURDER of Archbishop Becket shocked everbody. Miracles and miraculous cures were said to have happened almost immediately. Soon pilgrims or travellers came in large numbers to Canterbury to his shrine in the cathedral.

▲ *King Henry pays penance at Becket's tomb in the cathedral in 1174.*

IN 1173 the Pope made Becket a saint. Henry II was deeply sorry about the murder and came to the cathedral in 1174 to repent.

◀ *A pewter pilgrim badge showing an image of Becket*

A SERIOUS FIRE damaged the cathedral in 1174, which gave the monks an opportunity to build a great new choir. As part of this rebuilding project, Thomas was given a beautiful new shrine.

Over the next three hundred years, thousands of pilgrims visited the shrine and brought much wealth to Canterbury.

Becket's Shrine

THE COMING OF THE FRIARS

FRIARS WERE RELIGIOUS MEN BUT UNLIKE THE MONKS, THEY WENT INTO TOWNS TO PREACH TO PEOPLE ABOUT GOD.

THEY BEGGED for food and shelter as they were not supposed to own land or farms.

Kings, nobles, the archbishop and ordinary people all helped the friars. At the new friaries where they lived, the friars built very large churches. This allowed them to preach to many more people.

FINDS FROM RECENT ARCHAEOLOGICAL EXCAVATIONS OF FRIARY SITES IN CANTERBURY

Fragments of parchment found at Whitefriars

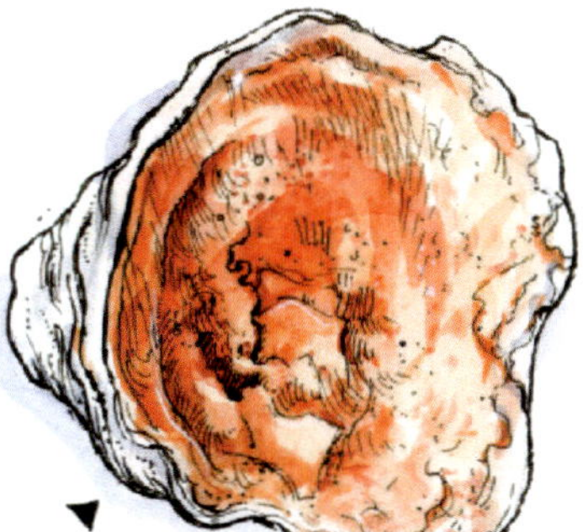

Oyster shell used as a painting palette

Lead papal seal

Stained glass fragment

ITEMS ENLARGED AND NOT TO SCALE

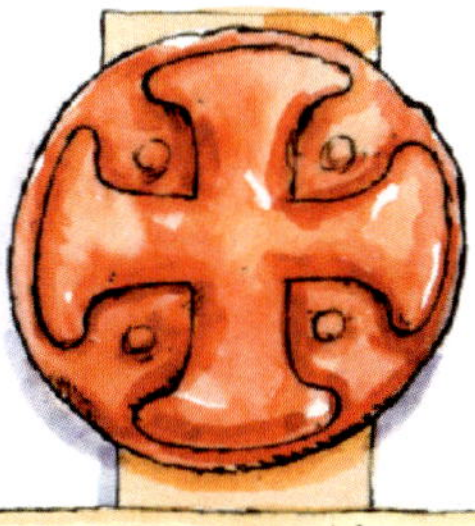

·DOMINICANS·

THE FIRST FRIARS to arrive in Canterbury in 1221 were the Dominicans – followers of a Spanish friar called St Dominic. These Black Friars (they wore black robes) started building their own friary buildings in 1236.

King Henry III helped them by giving money and oak trees.

·FRANCISCANS·

THE FRANCISCANS or Grey Friars were followers of St Francis of Assisi. When the first Franciscan friars arrived in Canterbury in 1224, they were helped by the brothers at the Poor Priests' Hospital in Stour Street. The brothers helped them build a chapel on an island behind the hospital.

There were other orders of friars in ENGLAND including the CARMELITE, PIED and CRUTCHED FRIARS.

·AUSTIN FRIARS·

A HUNDRED YEARS after the Dominicans and Franciscans, the Austin Friars arrived in Canterbury. They built their friary in the area now known as **Whitefriars**. This name was not used until after the friary had disappeared.

During the "BIG DIG" before the Whitefriars Shopping Centre was built, archaeologists found part of the friary church, several skeletons from the friary cemetery and a very large cess pit.

CHARTERS, COURTS, COINS AND CRIMINALS

CHARTERS

IN THE MIDDLE AGES Canterbury belonged to the King. His officials collected the taxes and organised the law courts. As time passed certain kings made agreements with the townsmen called charters.

In 1236 King Henry III made a charter which allowed the citizens of Canterbury to have their own law court.

THE BURMOTE HORN

To call men to the Burmote the Burmote horn was blown at special places in the city. Today it is still used on the day the Lord Mayor is appointed.

CANTERBURY'S COURT or **BURMOTE** (town meeting) met every fortnight. The most important elected officers were bailiffs. In the 15th century the city gained the right to elect a mayor instead of the bailiffs.

COURTS

Not everybody who lived in Canterbury was involved in these elections for the Burmote. The men who could were called Freemen. As well as the 'Burmote' for the city as a whole, there were 'Wardmotes' because the city was divided into six areas or wards.

Meeting of the Canterbury Burmote or city council

COINS

A FEW CITIZENS called moneyers had permission from the king to make coins. This meant Canterbury was special because in the 13th century only two other towns had this right.

CRIMINALS

THOSE FOUND GUILTY by the city court were punished. Not everybody was put in the pillory, some were fined, others put in the stocks. Those convicted of more serious crimes such as murder and theft were hanged on the gallows.

THE BLACK DEATH

THE GREAT MORTALITY (later called the Black Death) arrived in western England in 1348 and spread rapidly, reaching all parts of Kent by the end of the year and all of England by the end of 1349.

Symptoms included dark blotches on the skin, lumps like insect bites that swelled to become hardened, painful boils or "buboes" and a blackened tongue. Death often followed within a week.

THROUGHOUT ENGLAND ABOUT A THIRD OF THE POPULATION DIED! BUT DEATH RATES VARIED FROM PLACE TO PLACE

IN CANTERBURY, historical writings tell us that very few monks at St Augustine's Abbey or at Canterbury Cathedral died in the first outbreak.

WE DO NOT KNOW how many townspeople died in Canterbury, but at nearby Sandwich they had to enlarge the burial ground to take all the bodies. Though the most devastating, this was the first of many plague outbreaks in medieval Canterbury.

THE PEASANTS' REVOLT

THE BLACK DEATH must have been a terrible experience, but for the surviving wage earners it offered new opportunities. Wage rates increased. The king and nobles tried to keep them down. It led to hatred between most townspeople (wage earners) and the nobles and senior churchmen like the archbishop (wage payers).

Peasants free prisoners and burn records at the Castle Keep, Canterbury

DURING MUCH of the later 1300s England was at war with France. This was very expensive and to pay for it the government brought in a new sort of tax - the poll tax. As a result of all these problems in 1381 many peasants and townspeople rebelled, especially in Kent and Essex.

BEFORE heading for London the Kentish rebels under their leader Wat Tyler marched on Canterbury. Among the places they attacked were the castle and the Archbishop's Palace. The revolt was later put down by the king.

THE CANTERBURY TALES and CHAUCER'S CANTERBURY

GEOFFREY CHAUCER'S "The Canterbury Tales" is one of the most important books in the English language. It is a long poem about a group of pilgrims who told stories to pass the time whilst they were travelling from London to St Thomas's shrine at Canterbury Cathedral.

Chaucer died in 1400 before he could finish the poem.

Chaucer's pilgrims travelling to Canterbury

ENTERING CANTERBURY through the West Gate, pilgrims would have seen the gun loops and the portcullis. Having special openings through which soldiers could fire guns was new in 1380 when the West Gate was rebuilt and a very novel design.

It was part of the city's rebuilt defences after war broke out again between England and France in 1369.

Pilgrims entering through the West Gate

THE OTHER major buildings constructed in Canterbury in the 1300s were inns.

Pilgrims and other travellers stayed in inns like the Cheker of the Hope. The Cheker was built by the cathedral monks in 1392-5 at a cost then of £862. There were shops on the ground floor and two floors of dormitories and other rooms. The Crown Inn was next door. The two inns made up the whole of one side of Mercery Lane.

Pilgrims arriving at a Canterbury Inn

THE LATE MEDIEVAL CATHEDRAL

HENRY IV's TOMB

CANTERBURY CATHEDRAL has two royal tombs - those of the Black Prince and King Henry IV. Both tombs are close to the site of the shrine of St Thomas.

The Black Prince was a great warrior and armour and weapons were placed above his tomb. He died in 1376, the year before his father King Edward III.

TOMB OF THE BLACK PRINCE

The Black Prince's son, King Richard II, had the crown taken from him by his cousin who became King Henry IV, the first Lancastrian king.

SOME PARTS of the cathedral and the priory were rebuilt around the 1400s. The masons took down the old nave and finished rebuilding the new one in 1405. This is the nave we see today. It is built in the Perpendicular style - upright straight lines - so it is very tall. Sometimes sermons were preached in the nave and church courts were held there.

Other new additions included the pulpitum which is a carved stone screen between the choir (for the monks) and the nave. It contains statues of the kings. New stained glass was also produced showing the Yorkist King Edward IV and his family.

The great central tower called Bell Harry was finished by 1500.

Christ Church Gate about 1500.

THE NEW GATEWAY was completed in 1521. It was built to mark the marriage of Prince Arthur, the eldest son of King Henry VII, to Catherine of Aragon.

TOMB OF ARCHBISHOP CHICHELE

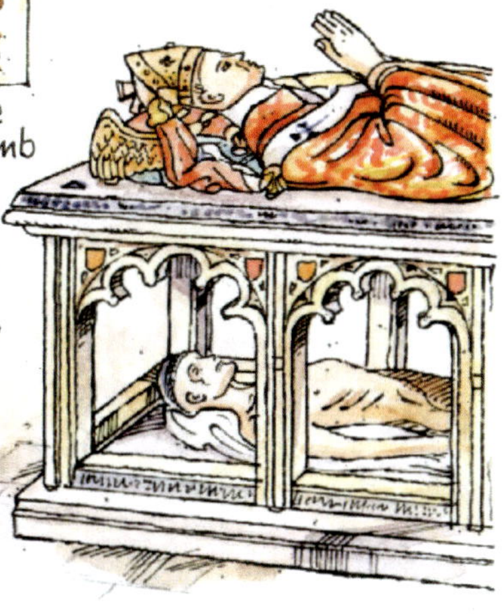

Archbishop Chichele designed his own tomb before his death.

He wanted people to remember that he was an archbishop and also an ordinary man.

HENRY VIII and the Dissolution of the Monasteries

▲ *On Henry VIII's orders valuables are removed from the Cathedral in 1538.*

AFTER PRINCE ARTHUR, Henry VII's eldest son died, Arthur's brother Henry married Catherine of Aragon. Queen Catherine and King Henry VIII at first were happily married but the king wanted a son to follow him and none of Catherine's baby sons survived. They had a daughter who would later become Queen Mary I. Henry then fell in love with Anne Boleyn. Henry wanted to divorce Catherine but the Pope would not agree to this.

Henry VIII

HENRY BECAME DESPERATE, seeking help from Thomas Cromwell his chancellor and Thomas Cranmer his archbishop. Together they agreed on a plan. Even though there was considerable opposition, great changes took place regarding how the Catholic Church in England was organised.

ONE OF THESE CHANGES WAS THAT IN 1534 KING HENRY DECLARED THAT HE, NOT THE POPE, WAS THE HEAD OF THE CHURCH IN ENGLAND – THE ANGLICAN CHURCH. AS A RESULT HENRY GOT HIS DIVORCE AND MARRIED ANNE BOLEYN.

TWO YEARS LATER, Henry's officials went around England closing the religious houses and taking their possessions for the Crown. At Canterbury Cathedral Henry declared St Thomas a banned saint. All the precious gifts given by pilgrims at St Thomas's shrine were broken up, loaded on carts and taken to London.

BECAUSE OF ITS MANY CHURCH BUILDINGS AND COMMUNITIES, CANTERBURY WAS SEEN AS A POTENTIAL SITE OF CATHOLIC RESISTANCE TO HENRY'S REFORMS.

IN 1538 the king took over St Augustine's Abbey and started altering the buildings. Later others were demolished. Some of the stone was taken to Calais to build the defences there. Other stone was sold to people in Canterbury for their own buildings. What remained of St Augustine's Abbey became a Royal Palace. At the cathedral, with the monastery gone, Henry set up the Dean and Chapter in 1541. Of the former monks, 28 joined the new religious community. The many friaries also disappeared around this time.

Henry VIII visiting his new palace in Canterbury

AFTER the wrecking of St Thomas's shrine and the disappearance of many religious buildings, Canterbury's pilgrim trade dried up and this meant great hardship for the city.

CHRISTOPHER MARLOWE – Playwright and Spy?

CHRISTOPHER MARLOWE was born in 1564 in St George's parish in Canterbury. William Shakespeare was born the same year. Marlowe's father was a shoemaker and moderately well-off. Christopher was lucky and very bright – he won a scholarship to attend the Kings School in the grounds of Canterbury Cathedral. Later he won another scholarship to study at Cambridge.

Schooling in Marlowe's time

The tower of the church in which Marlowe was christened – St George's can still be seen today at the top of the High Street.

AFTER HIS studies, he went to London. Performing drama in an actual theatre building was a new idea. People before that had seen plays in yards, streets or great halls. Marlowe wrote plays for the London theatre that were very popular. One of the most famous was about Dr Faustus. In the opening scene Dr Faustus is in his study, which might have been like the study of his old headmaster at Canterbury.

Marlowe also wrote poems.

A performance of 'Dr Faustus' at a London theatre

MARLOWE DIED young aged only 29. He was killed at a house in Deptford during a quarrel on the 30th May 1593. An inquest was held because it was a violent death, but there are still many unanswered questions about what happened that evening. He may have been involved in spying.

BECAUSE he died young, he only wrote a few plays, whereas William Shakespeare (who may have been influenced by Marlowe's plays) lived longer and wrote far more. Marlowe remains, however, one of England's greatest playwrights.

"Was this the face that launched a thousand ships?" – 'Dr Faustus'

"Come live with me and be my love and we will all the pleasures prove" – 'The Passionate Shepherd.'

ELIZABETHAN CANTERBURY

Elizabeth I dines in the Archbishop's Hall

THE RELIGIOUS CHANGES during the reigns of Queen Elizabeth's father (Henry VIII), brother (Edward VI) and sister (Mary I) made life difficult for many people in Canterbury.

Work was scarce, because pilgrims did not visit Canterbury anymore and some industries such as cloth-making moved to the countryside. Many people were poor but a few wealthy townsmen built grand houses out of the ruins of the religious houses. Whitefriars became an Elizabethan mansion with formal gardens.

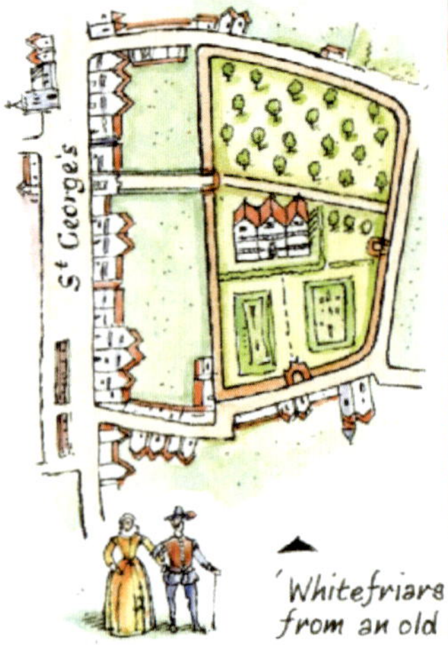

'Whitefriars House' from an old map

THE CITY was in a poor state with some houses fallen down and people dumped rubbish in the city ditch. However, Queen Elizabeth I came to Canterbury to celebrate her 40th birthday in 1573.

She stayed at the royal palace on the site of the now dissolved St Augustine's Abbey. During her stay she went to dinner at the Archbishop of Canterbury's great hall.

CANTERBURY'S WEAVERS

THE WALLOONS were people from the southern Netherlands and northern France. They were Protestants who came to Canterbury in 1575 to escape religious persecution.
They spoke French and many of them were skilled at making cloth.
They mainly wove from a mixture of wool, linen and silk to make "the new draperies" as such materials were called.
This helped revive Canterbury's trade.

There are several houses remaining in Canterbury today that were built during the Elizabethan period.

◄ This one is in the High Street.

Townspeople did not spend all their time working or going to church. Some went to watch plays, or practice archery, others watched cock-fighting and dancing bears.

One man was fined for taking his bear onto the city wall!

EARLY STUART CANTERBURY

By 1600 around 6,000 people lived in Canterbury. Maybe as many as a third were refugees who spoke French. They contributed a lot to the city economy.

County gentlemen started to acquire town houses in Canterbury. At Baron Wotton's house, on the site of St Augustine's Abbey, John Tradescant the elder, soon to be the King's gardener, created a magnificent formal garden with exotic plants – melons, mandrakes and pomegranates.

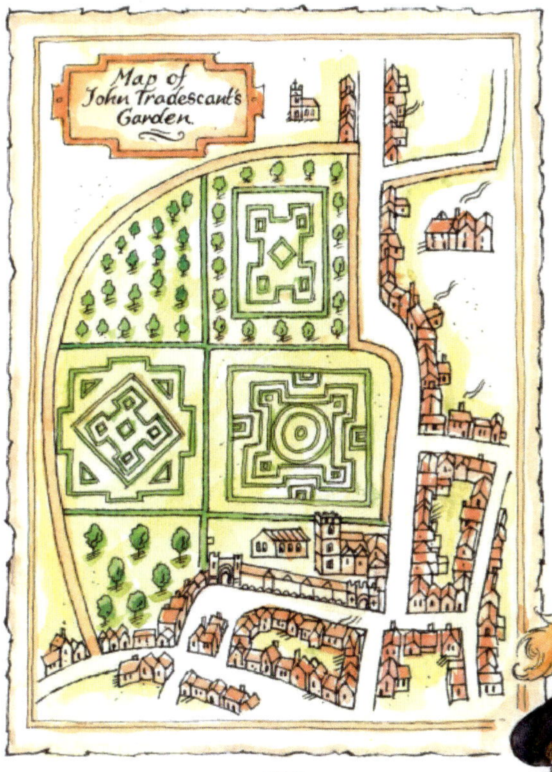

Canterbury Christ Church University now occupies most of Tradescant's garden.

On 13th June 1625 Charles I welcomed his French bride to England. They spent their first night together in Canterbury.

Charles became increasingly unpopular. Householders in Canterbury disobeyed his orders to put up soldiers in their homes. They also disliked high taxes.

JOHN FINCH the Speaker of the House of Commons, came from Canterbury. In 1629 the King asked him to adjourn Parliament but fellow MPs stopped him. They held him down in the Speaker's chair.

There is a memorial to John Finch in St Martin's church.

VOYAGES TO A NEW WORLD

ROBERT CUSHMAN was a city grocer, often in trouble with the church. In 1608 he emigrated to Holland. When a group of English exiles left Holland for America in 1620, Cushman helped organise their voyage on the Mayflower.

Even more people emigrated in the 1630s. They disapproved of religious changes introduced by Archbishop Laud of Canterbury. Around forty of these emigrants were from Canterbury. **EDWARD JOHNSON**, a joiner, undertook the six-week voyage with his wife Susan and seven young children – a nerve-wracking experience.

CIVIL WAR!

From 1629 to 1640 Charles I ruled without Parliament. When he recalled MPs, they refused to grant him any money unless he met popular demands. The King refused to compromise and civil war broke out.

A 1642 petition supporting Parliament was signed by 185 people in Canterbury ▶

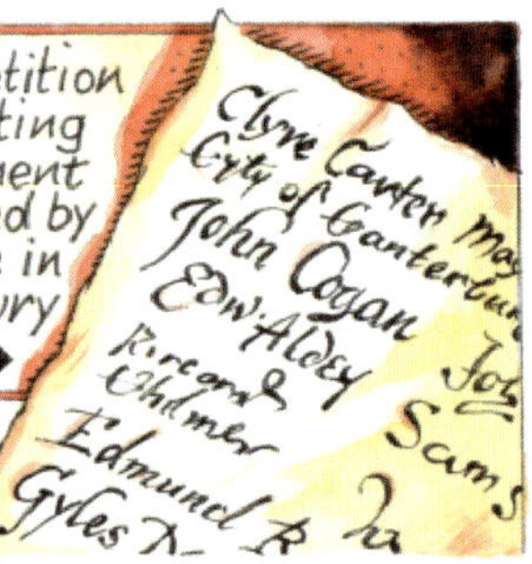

Some MPs just wanted the King to co-operate with them. But others wanted radical religious reform. They ordered the destruction of religious images. Stained-glass windows in Canterbury Cathedral were smashed, the statue of Jesus was pulled down from the Christchurch Gate, and the market cross was removed.

There was even talk of demolishing the cathedral!

Rev. Richard Culmer, 'rattling down proud Becket's glassie bones' in Canterbury Cathedral ▼

In 1647 Parliament banned Christmas celebrations and ordered shops to open as usual. This led to riots in Canterbury. Goods were swept off market stalls. The Sheriff's head was 'fearfully broke'. A holly bush, symbolising Christmas, was left outside the Mayor's house. A rampaging mob chanted 'For God, King Charles and Kent'. County authorities sent troops to breach the walls and burn down the gates.

The Canterbury riots triggered a second round of the English Civil War. After a bloody battle at Maidstone, Parliamentary troops marched here. The city surrendered and some 3,000 weapons were laid down at the cathedral.

AFTER THE WAR

When Charles visited, there was still a steeple on the cathedral's north-west tower. It was taken down after the great storm of 1703.

In 1660 Charles II returned to England after years of exile, greeted by cheering crowds. He spent the first weekend of his reign in Canterbury and assembled his Privy Council here. The Mayor presented him with a golden tankard, full of coins, worth £250. William Somner, author of *The Antiquities of Canterbury*, gave the King a copy of his book.

HUGUENOT REFUGEES

In 1685 a new wave of Protestant refugees fled persecution in France. Some arrived with nothing but the clothes they escaped in. But skilled silk-weavers and paper-makers soon found work.

Within a few years, Canterbury's silk industry began to decline as silks were imported from other countries. Many Huguenot families moved to London. Others became a permanent part of Canterbury society.

ILLEGAL MEETINGS

Several congregations of religious dissenters had grown up in the 1640s and 50s. Charles' Parliament banned religious services outside the Church of England.

Some people were imprisoned for attending dissenting meetings.

Dissenters were not allowed to worship freely until 1689.

SNAPSHOTS OF THE 1700s

NEWSPAPER

Kent's first newspaper, *The Kentish Post or Canterbury Newsletter* (1717-1768) was published in Canterbury. Most of its news concerned London but it carried local advertisements and hop prices.

THE
Kentish POST:
OR,
Canterbury News-letter

From WEDNESDAY December 19, to SATURDAY December 22, 1722

Daniel Defoe

HOP GARDENS

During the 1700s hop-farming became Canterbury's main industry. When Daniel Defoe, author of 'Robinson Crusoe', visited in 1724 he was amazed by *'the most surprising increase in hop-gardens'.* Many tradesmen cultivated an acre or two in addition to their main jobs. Each hop-vine was grown up its own pole.

ELECTIONS

Elections took place in the Guild (Town) Hall, which stood in the High Street until the 1950s. According to Gostling, voters went up one staircase and down another to avoid crowding each other. They had to say out loud who they were voting for. Candidates often bribed them with beer.

WATER SUPPLY

In 1733 Sir John Hales paid for new pipes and improved the city's water supply.

Householders got their water from communal pumps, such as the Red Pump at the junction of Sun and Palace Streets.

William Gostling

Author of 'A Walk in and About the City of Canterbury' (1774)

John Wesley

METHODISTS

John Wesley, a famous travelling preacher, visited Canterbury nearly every year for 40 years. On his first visit in 1750, people came to hear him before work at 5am. Wesley was very methodical so his followers became known as 'Methodists'. In 1764 they opened a chapel in King Street, nicknamed the Pepper Box because of its shape.

RECREATION

By 1750 there were around a hundred inns in Canterbury. Some hosted flower shows, 'Auricula Feasts', with dinner, and prizes for the best polyanthus.

Some inns had their own cock pits. 'Gentlemen of Canterbury' staged fights against teams from neighbouring towns. There was also a cock pit at St Augustine's Abbey – along with a bowling green, fives court, and skittle yard.

From the 1730s the Canterbury races were held every summer on Barham Downs. The main prize, the King's Plate, was worth 100 guineas. The races became a major social occasion with assemblies and dances.

In 1765 the *Kentish Post* announced that on Thursday 25th July 'Master Mozart, the celebrated German Boy aged eight years' would perform at the Town Hall. Admission was 2s 6d, between £8 and £9 in today's money.

The THEATRE

The theatre in the Buttermarket probably looked like this.

The top floor of the Market Hall in the Buttermarket served as a theatre. When the building was demolished in 1789, a resourceful actress, Mrs Sarah Baker, built her own theatre in Orange Street, now the Merchant Chandler.

CATCH & GLEE CLUB

A Catch and Glee Club met on Wednesdays at the Prince of Orange pub. Members drank beer or punch, smoked pipes, sang catches (rounds), and listened to an orchestra, led by the landlord, John Goodban. His wife sang solos (and served meat pies). Later the club got its own building.

CRIME and PUNISHMENT

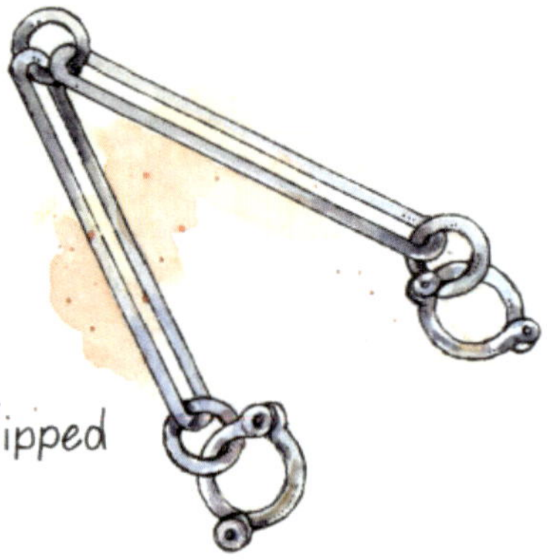

In June 1773 Jane Calman, 'an idle and disorderly person', and William Page, who had stolen a tea-kettle, were whipped 'at the cart's tail' from West Gate to St George's Gate.

Whipping was a common 18th-century punishment.

Some offenders were fined. In 1790 the Mayor fined two people five shillings for failing to sweep the pavement in front of their houses.

Sometimes criminals were transported to other countries. In 1789 John Kirby was sentenced to seven-years transportation for stealing four geese.

Canterbury had two prisons, a city gaol in the West Gate and a county gaol in St Dunstan's Street, replaced in 1808 by a new building opposite Barton Court. Most prison terms were short. In 1795 Mary Crighton, a widow, was imprisoned for 14 days for stealing a silver spoon.

"Daniel Dilnot May being now charged on the Coroners Inquest for Manslaughter – pleads not Guilty and is by the Jury found not Guilty and is Acquitted –"

The prison today

Death sentences were rare, often altered to transportation. Until the 1790s there was a gallows at Oaten Hill. When Margaret Hughes was hanged in 1799 for poisoning her husband, a temporary scaffold was erected outside the West Gate gaol. Her body was given to surgeons for dissection.

In 1802 two soldiers were hanged at the West Gate for highway robbery on the Sturry Road. The *Kentish Gazette* said it was the first double hanging in the city since 1633.

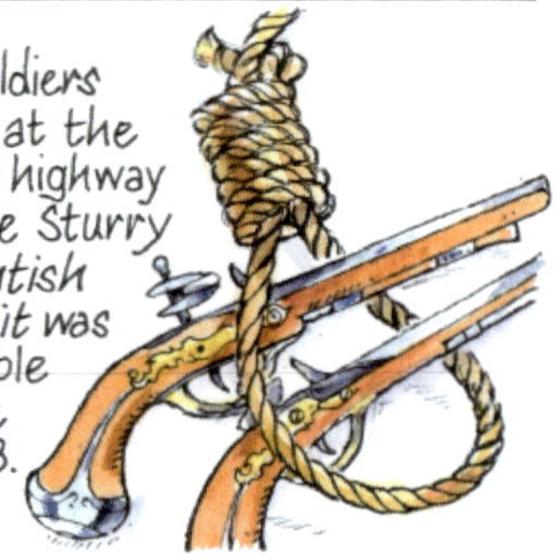

GEORGIAN ELEGANCE

Alderman James Simmons, 'Canterbury's Great Tycoon', was born and educated in the city. A stationer and printer, he founded the *Kentish Gazette* in 1768, and later expanded into banking and milling. Twice mayor, he was elected MP just before he died.

Simmons took the lead in making Canterbury a cleaner, more elegant city. In 1787 an act of Parliament gave commissioners draconian powers to pave, straighten and improve the city's streets. Around 40 householders were ordered to cut back windows which projected beyond the foundations of their houses.

▲ *James Simmons (1741–1807) with plans for a canal from Canterbury to the sea*

MATHEMATICAL TILES ▼

As timber-framed houses went out of fashion, new brick frontages were put on to old buildings. Some people used 'mathematical tiles', which looked like bricks.

Carriages had difficulty navigating narrow medieval streets. Simmons helped finance a new road, Guildhall Street. The old city gates were taken down. Only West Gate, which housed the city gaol, survived – due to high demolition costs.

▲ *According to the Kentish Traveller's Companion 'from being one of the worst paved cities', Canterbury became one of the best.*

THE DANE JOHN

Simmons was a major city benefactor. He spent over £1,500 transforming the Dane John from rough pastureland into landscaped gardens for popular use. Money was raised by public subscription to erect a monument to him on the Dane John Mound. ▶

Jane Austen probably strolled through the Dane John Gardens when visiting her brother.

THE BARRACKS

In the 1790s, as part of national precautions against French invasion, huge new barracks were built along the Sturry Road. Most of the vast complex was demolished between 1967 and 1972 but the garrison church, All Saints, still stands. So does the soldiers' theatre, now Northgate Community Centre.

By 1809 there were 3,750 soldiers in Canterbury and stabling for 1,080 horses. The resident population of the city and suburbs was under 12,000.

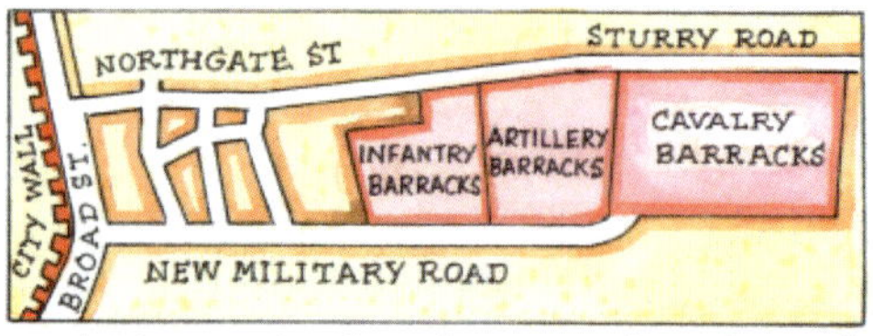

▲ 1843 map showing closeness of the barracks to the city

1st Royal Dragoon

Soldiers drank in city pubs such as The Royal Dragoon in Military Road, The Ordnance Arms, and the Gun Tavern.

The barracks provided much local employment. Builders and labourers were constantly on call. Tradesmen supplied goods from food to footwear.

Soldiers had a big impact on Canterbury. Over a hundred different regiments came and went, parading through the streets in colourful regalia. The Royal East Kent Regiment (the Buffs) developed a special relationship with the city.

Royal East Kent

Women earned money as servants, washerwomen, and prostitutes. Boys were paid to remove vast quantities of dung.

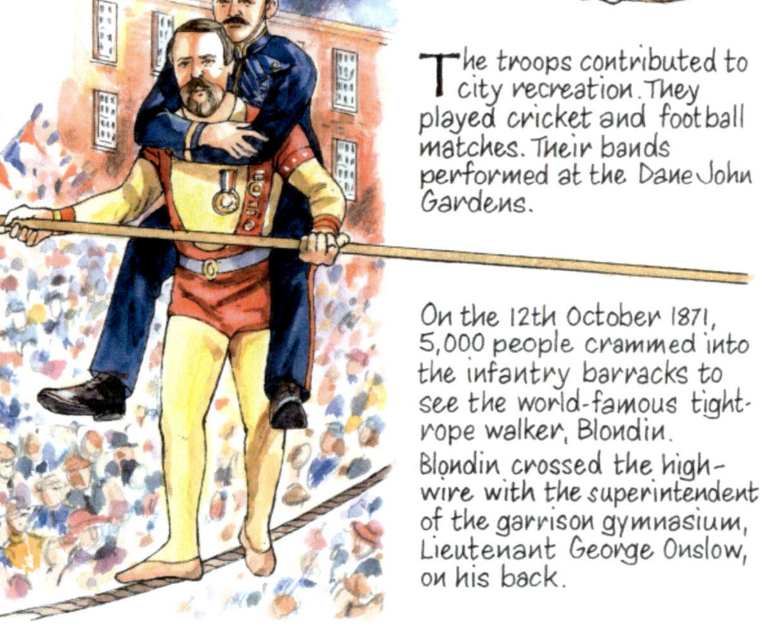

The troops contributed to city recreation. They played cricket and football matches. Their bands performed at the Dane John Gardens.

On the 12th October 1871, 5,000 people crammed into the infantry barracks to see the world-famous tightrope walker, Blondin.

Blondin crossed the high-wire with the superintendent of the garrison gymnasium, Lieutenant George Onslow, on his back.

ROADS & RAILWAYS

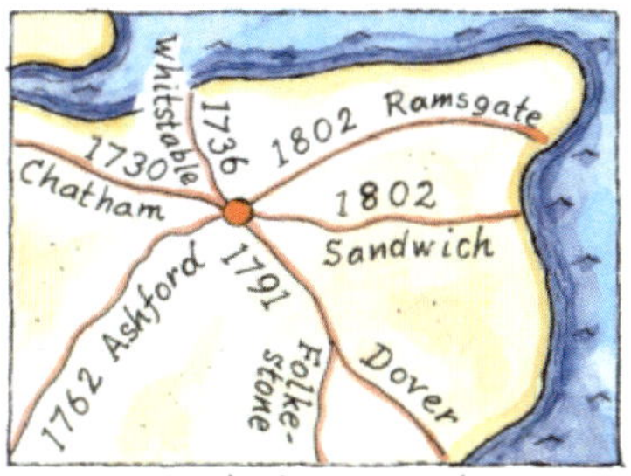

▲ Toll roads to Canterbury

Eighteenth-century roads were dreadful, so trusts were created to improve and maintain them. Travellers paid tolls at newly erected toll-gates, including one outside St Dunstan's church. Between 1730 and 1802 tolls were established on six routes into Canterbury.

The journey by stagecoach from London took around 11 hours.

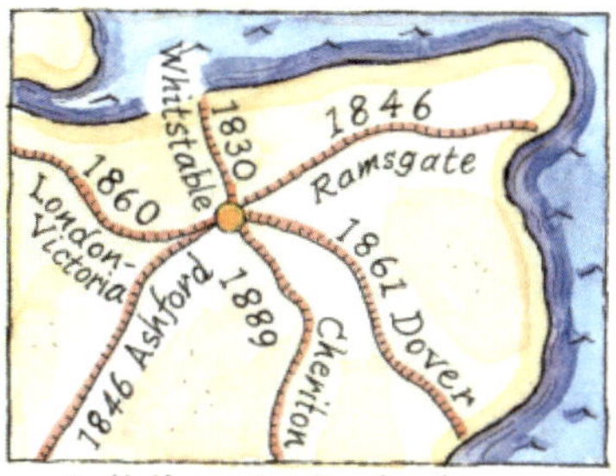

▲ Rail lines to Canterbury

The Canterbury-Whitstable railway opened on 3rd May 1830 (four and a half months before the Liverpool-Manchester line). Two stationary engines hauled excited passengers by ropes and pulleys up inclines and through an 828-yard tunnel. A moving engine, or 'loco-motive', the 'INVICTA', was only used on the Whitstable stretch.

In 1834 the company issued the world's first 'season' tickets (price 2 guineas, 5 for families), valid during the sea-bathing season – (25 March to 1 November).

◀ Roadside milestone to Canterbury

▲ Approaching Whitstable

In Arthur Conan Doyle's story, 'The Final Problem', published in 1893, Sherlock Holmes and Watson are chased across south-east England by train. They escape Professor Moriarty by getting off at Canterbury East station.

Rival companies constructed three competing railway lines, each with its own station. 'Canterbury West' (originally Canterbury Station) opened in 1846, the 'East' station (almost due south of it) in 1860, and 'Canterbury South' in 1889. This third station, where the Kent and Canterbury hospital now stands, served the Elham Valley line.

◀ *Robert Stephenson's 'INVICTA' now in the Canterbury Museum.*

THE 1830s

The 1830s were tumultuous years. On 28th August 1830 labourers destroyed threshing machines at Lower Hardres, just outside Canterbury, the first of many attacks. Corn was traditionally threshed by hand. The new machines deprived farm workers of winter employment.

The Kentish Gazette attributed machine-breaking to 'great and dire distress.' At first magistrates imposed light sentences, just a few days imprisonment. As destruction continued, punishments became harsher, including transportation.

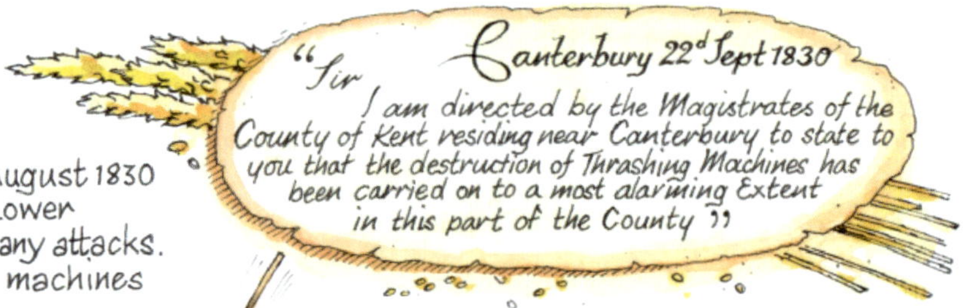

◂ Archbishop William Howley

▴ Threshing with a flail

▴ Threshing with machine

In December 1832 there was a general election. A charismatic, flamboyantly dressed, mentally unstable Cornishman, John Toms, stood for election in Canterbury. Toms claimed to be Sir William Courtenay, Knight of Malta.

379 people out of an electorate of 1,511 voted for him. ▾

The great issue of the day was parliamentary reform. Canterbury's two aristocratic MPs supported reform but Archbishop Howley opposed it. When he visited the city in August 1832 a hissing crowd pelted his carriage with cabbage stalks.

THE BATTLE OF BOSENDEN WOOD

The winter of 1838 was very harsh and poor relief inadequate. Courtenay proclaimed 'an end to the oppression of the poor by the rich.' To poverty-stricken farm labourers he appeared a messianic figure.

His supporters marched round the countryside, carrying a loaf of bread on a stick. Soldiers were sent in after Courtenay killed a man who was trying to arrest him. He died in what became known as 'the battle of Bosenden Wood' along with eight of his followers.

POVERTY and PUBLIC HEALTH

Before the welfare state, charity was a major means of relieving poverty. £4,496 was raised by public subscription for a hospital for the 'sick and lame poor from any part of the County'. The Kent and Canterbury Hospital opened in Longport in 1793 (and moved to its present site in 1937).

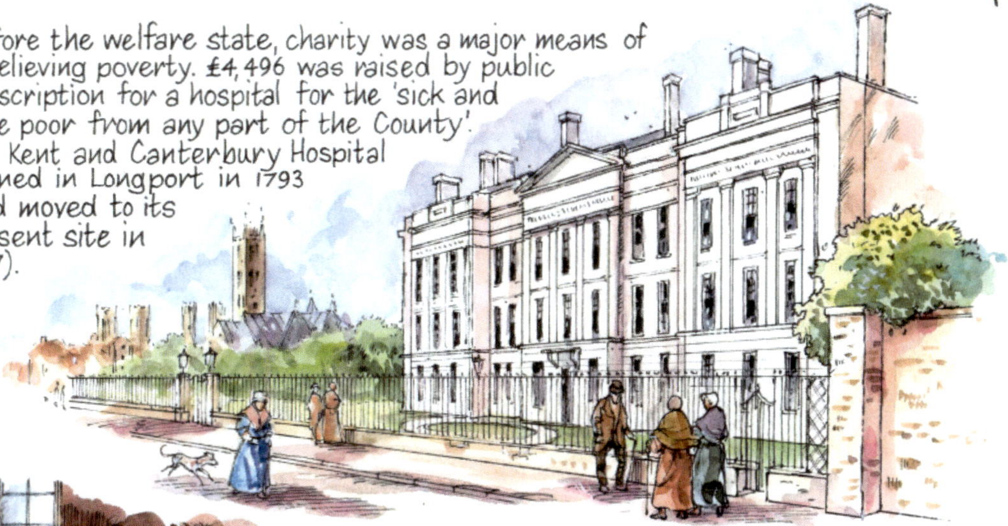

In 1794 James Hiett left funds for ten woollen coats a year for 'aged and infirm men' over 50. In harsh winters and bad harvests, mayors collected money to buy bread for the hungry.

Rates were levied to relieve the poor, sometimes at home, often in workhouses. Workhouse life was regimented. Inmates did jobs such as making hop bags. The Poor Priests' Hospital was turned into a workhouse in 1727. A new one opened in Nunnery Fields in 1849.

Poor areas such as Northgate were very crowded. In 1847 39 adults and 43 children lived in 26 rooms, sharing one pump and one privy.

Canterbury was an unhealthy city, full of slaughter-house waste and pig muck. Cess pools filled the air with 'offensive smells' and 'poisonous exhalations'. Privies and sewers emptied into the river, which sometimes overflowed. Although new drains were built in the 1860s, the council massively cut costs and problems continued. Death rates were high, particularly near the river.

MADE IN CANTERBURY

By Victoria's reign Canterbury's weaving industry had declined but another old trade, hop-farming, flourished. Local people picked hops in fields right next to the city. The Wesleyan Day School started the autumn term, 1871, a week late 'owing to hopping being still unfinished'.

BREWING

Canterbury had at least ten breweries, including one run by the appropriately named George Beer.

Another big brewery, Flint and Sons, stretched right up St Dunstan's Street.

MILLING

Many mills operated along the River Stour, notably the six-storey Abbot's Mill erected by James Simmons. This remained in use until it burnt down in 1933.

TANNING LEATHER

St Mildred's Tannery was run by the Williamson family. People still remember the smell! In 1938 Catherine Williamson became Canterbury's first female mayor. The Williamsons donated their home, Tower House, to the city.

·IRONWORKS·

A family firm, Bigglestons, had an iron foundry in the heart of Canterbury (by today's Nasons). Bigglestons made lamp-posts which can still be seen all over the city - and the clock on St George's Tower. The firm supplied iron-work for railways, constructed the first torpedo (which exploded on test at Herne Bay), and produced the first tin fountain pen.

Pouring molten iron into a mould

WINDMILLS AND MACHINERY

Holmans, a family firm based in Dover Street, built many local windmills, including one at Sarre. They even constructed a mill in Jerusalem, commissioned by Sir Moses Montefiore. This was subsequently depicted on Israeli stamps and banknotes. As steam replaced wind, Holmans diversified into agricultural machinery. They hired out traction engines to local farmers.

Windmill in Jerusalem, 1857 – made in Canterbury and still standing

RELIGION

CHURCH-GOING

Victorian congregations were much bigger than today's. A religious census recorded that on 30th March 1851, 828 people attended evening worship at St Peter's Street Wesleyan Chapel, the best attended service in Canterbury.

THE JEWISH COMMUNITY

When the synagogue at St Dunstan's was demolished for the Canterbury West railway, the Jewish community erected a new, Egyptian-style building in King Street.

By now Jews were an accepted part of society. A leading member of the congregation, businessman and Freemason Henry Hart, served three times as Mayor of Canterbury.

SUNDAY SCHOOLS

On 22nd June 1897, the Queen's Diamond Jubilee, over 4,000 children from Sunday Schools and Boys' Brigades processed to the Cricket Ground for a free tea, games and entertainment.

Some of the grounds of St Augustine's Abbey had become a pleasure garden. In 1844 churchmen, shocked by fireworks and dancing, bought the site for a missionary college.

▲ *Kallihirua 1856*

Students from overseas included an Inuit, Erasmus Augustine Kallihirua, and a Zulu, Gregory Ngcobo.

Some graduates died young, soon after reaching the mission field. Their names are recorded on plaques in the college chapel, now part of King's School.

▲ *Gregory Ngcobo 1895*

The Salvation Army developed as a mission to non-churchgoers. With its brass bands, military uniforms, and female preachers, it attracted a lot of hostility. But in 1886 crowds flocked to its first meeting in Canterbury, curious to hear two 'hallelujah lasses' preaching.

In 1880 Jesuits opened a college on the Hales Place Estate, along what is now The Terrace.

RAGS TO RICHES

Thomas Sidney Cooper (1803-1902)

Sidney Cooper's father abandoned his family. His mother worked as a dressmaker to support five children. One day Archbishop Manners Sutton saw the boy drawing and paid him £5 for a picture. Cooper became a famous artist, specialising in cattle. Queen Victoria commissioned him to paint her favourite cow.

266 of his pictures were exhibited at the Royal Academy.

After his mother died, Cooper converted her cottage into an Art School to honour her and provide others with 'facilities I had been denied in my youth'.

One of his students was Canterbury-born Mary Caldwell, the daughter of a stained-glass restorer. As **Mary Tourtel** she created the newspaper strip Rupert Bear.

▲ *Mary Tourtel (1874 - 1948) as a young woman*

James George Beaney (1828-1891)

Beaney's father, a labourer, died when he was two. James worked hard to improve himself. He impressed early employers so much that he was apprenticed to Sidney Cooper's brother, an apothecary surgeon. After qualifying in Edinburgh, he emigrated to Australia, where he made a lot of money. Fellow doctors envied and disliked him. He was accused-and acquitted-of murdering a patient.

He published on sexual diseases.

◀ *The Beaney Institute for the Education of Working Men*

James Beaney as a young man ▶

Beaney left £10,000 for a free library and reading room in his native city.

He also left money for cathedral repairs-and a large memorial tablet to himself ▶

LEISURE and SPORT

Mineral springs had been discovered in Canterbury in 1693 but unlike those at Tunbridge Wells only attracted a few visitors.

In the 19th Century the wells became part of an exotic nursery garden, now Pound Lane car park. ▸

Canterbury's Philosophical and Literary Institution opened in Guildhall Street in 1825, with a library, and weekly lectures on literary, scientific and historical subjects. ▾

The Theatre Royal was next door. By the time the musical comedy, 'The Lady Cyclist', was performed there in 1899 Canterbury had its own cycling club. ▸

On 4th November 1861 Charles Dickens gave a two-hour reading from *David Copperfield* in the newly-opened Theatre Royal. He praised the accoustics and called the audience 'the most delicate..... I have seen in any provincial place'. ▸

In 1909 a roller skating rink was opened in the city.

Canterbury's first cricket ground was the Beverley at St Stephens. The St Lawrence Ground opened in 1847. Cricket Week was an important feature of the city calendar. On Ladies Day 1881 between eight and nine thousand people watched a Kentish twelve beat an All-England twelve.

There were always county balls during Cricket Week and performances by the Old Stagers, thought to be the world's oldest surviving amateur dramatic society.

From 1876 there was a public swimming pool in what is now Toddlers' Cove. Until 1939 schools held swimming competitions there.

CHANGING TIMES

By the 1890s some 23,000 people lived in Canterbury and its suburbs. New department stores such as Lefevres (now Debenhams) had opened alongside lots of small family-run shops. In 1885 the *Kentish Gazette* described Finns in St Margaret's Street as 'one of the largest and most complete trading establishments of the kind in the whole of England'.

By the end of the century all children had to attend school – up to the age of 12. Each year a few elementary-school pupils won scholarships to the Simon Langton Schools. These opened on the Whitefriars site in 1881.

Cars appeared on Canterbury streets in the early 20th century. Barretts, a family firm which still exists, was founded in 1902.

The city had been lit by gas since the 1820s. In 1898 an Electric Light Works was constructed near Northgate. Canterbury's first purpose-built Electric Theatre (cinema) opened in St Peter's Street in 1911.

Despite all these changes, Canterbury remained a small market town. Farmers brought livestock to sell at its cattle market, just outside the city walls.

Not everyone welcomed change. As late as 1882 the Dean and Chapter refused to set the cathedral clock to 'railway' (Greenwich) time. In 1887, after a bitter debate, the city council voted against funds for a telephone service. Critics deemed it unnecessary in 'a little stationary town like Canterbury.'

WORLD WAR 1

Canterbury was celebrating Cricket Week when war was declared on 4th August 1914. The famous Kent cricketer, Colin Blythe, volunteered immediately. He was killed three years later.

Lord Kitchener of Broome Park, Barham, was appointed War Minister. Public meetings at the Theatre Royal and Guild Hall appealed for volunteers for his 'New Army'. By 1916, 36 out of 62 employees at Finns store had joined the forces.

The Kentish Gazette collected money to send cigarettes, tobacco and Christmas puddings to soldiers at the front.

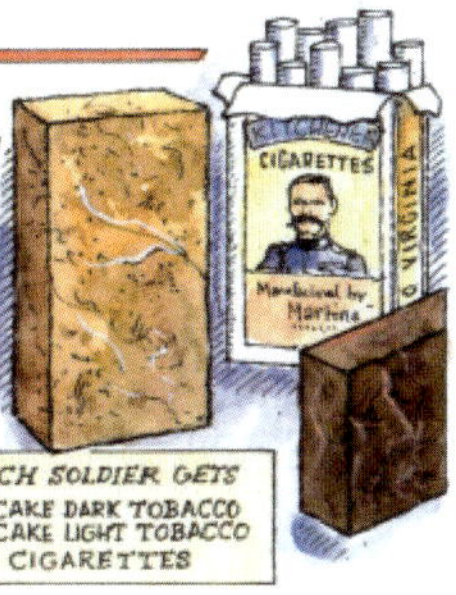

Wounded soldiers, including many Belgians, were brought to Canterbury. As the Kent and Canterbury Hospital did not have enough beds, Francis Bennett Goldney MP and the Misses Wightwick lent their homes, Abbots Barton and Dane John House.

Women joined Voluntary Aid Detachments to help with hospital duties. Around 60 women worked as land girls on Canterbury farms.

To help deal with food shortages, 243 allotments were created in the city.

Canterbury did not suffer air raids itself but on the 7th December 1917 a huge Gotha bomber crashed in Broad Oak.

Over 500 Canterbury men died in the war. On 10th October 1921 Field-Marshal the Earl Haig unveiled a memorial to them in the Buttermarket.

THE BLITZ OF CANTERBURY

In World War II German bombers used the Baedeker guidebook to Great Britain to target historic towns. People in Canterbury knew they would be bombed.

130 high explosives and 3,600 incendiaries fell just after midnight on 1st June 1942 in 'an hour and a quarter of unmitigated terror'. A cathedral fire-watcher saw one bomb miss Bell Harry Tower by just a few feet.

Over 3,000 buildings were destroyed or damaged. Simon Langton pupil, Ted Chappell, went to his school, 'and there it was - gone!' Many shopkeepers lost their premises. Luckier firms lent them floor space so they could continue trading.

▲ *The Corn and Hop Exchange in the Longmarket was one of the historic buildings lost in the blitz.*

697 people were made homeless. June Holmes was six. She recalled 'the whole house was burned down'. The rabbit hutch in the yard had caught fire but it was amazing the little rabbit was still sitting, all singed, in the corner'.

Bombs fell on Canterbury 35 times between 1940 and 1944. 115 people were killed and 380 injured. Michael Powell's 1944 film 'A Canterbury Tale' showed the devastated city.

Many families had steel Morrison shelters in their front rooms.

Others used air raid shelters in gardens. As raids continued some people felt safer sleeping away from town in the fields.

POST-WAR DEVELOPMENT

LONGMARKET LATE **1940s**

There were many arguments about the rebuilding of Canterbury. Councillors who supported an ambitious redevelopment plan were roundly defeated in the 1945 local elections.

For ten years there were prefabricated shops in the Longmarket. The box-shaped buildings which replaced them were themselves demolished 30 years later. Other new buildings, notably the David Greig shop facing Canterbury Lane, were more striking.

LONGMARKET **1961**

Traffic from London to Dover used to go right through Canterbury. Dual carriageways were built in the 1960s south and east of the city but plans for a full ring road were never realised.

DAVID GREIG'S **1953**

Slum housing was pulled down. So were some historic buildings such as the Guildhall.

The old moat walk outside the city walls gave way to a dual carriageway.

In 1953 post-war gloom was relieved by the coronation of Queen Elizabeth II. Street parties were held.

A huge crown on the Dane John memorial was lit up at night and the city's history was celebrated in a pageant.

1960s

Higher education brought new life and jobs to Canterbury. Christ Church College of Education (now Canterbury Christ Church University) opened in 1962 and the University of Kent three years later. 'Canterbury is embarking on a new era' said a local councillor.

MODERN CITY

In the last half century a once provincial market town has become a World Heritage Site, packed with young people and tourists.

© Peter Firmin
Oliver Postgate

YOUNG PEOPLE

Canterbury has the highest percentage of students to residents in the country.

Children's television owed much to Canterbury. Ivor the Engine, Noggin the Nog, the Clangers, and Bagpuss were all created in a Blean barn by Oliver Postgate and Peter Firmin.

In the 1960s and 1970s local rock bands, such as Caravan, achieved world-wide fame with their innovative 'Canterbury Sound'. One album was entitled 'Blind Dog at St Dunstans'.

Pope John Paul II made history by visiting Canterbury on 29th May 1982. He drove through the city in a 'popemobile'.

VISITORS

TODAY Canterbury is more accessible than ever before. The channel tunnel agreement was signed in the Chapter House on 12th February 1986 in a ceremony attended by Prime Minister Margaret Thatcher and the French President, François Mitterand.

Canterbury Cathedral attracts around a million visitors each year. Overseas schoolchildren mingle with people from all over East Kent, who shop at the new Whitefriars centre or attend the state-of-the-art Marlowe theatre. Audiences travel miles to the Canterbury Festival and other events.

Visitors from London can get here now in under an hour by high speed train. Using Eurostar, travellers from Paris can reach Canterbury within 3 hours.

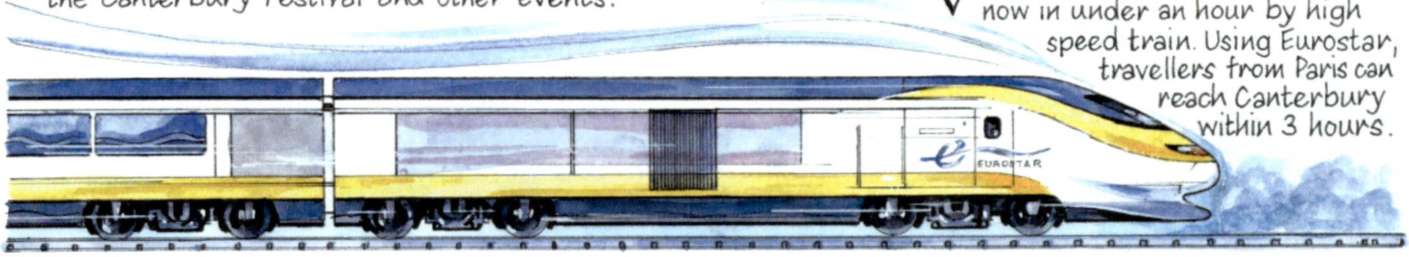